Lucky Feels Fuzzy

Written by Josie Martinez

Dedicated to my parents for doing their best.

Also dedicated to all the fuzzy people and their families.

Lucky the kitten was playing outside on a beautiful day when suddenly...

"Mommy I feel fuzzy." says Lucky as he goes to the kitchen to tell his mom. His front paws are falling asleep.

Lucky's mom already knows what's going on. His mom stops what she is doing and goes over to him. "My face feels fuzzy too."

His mom goes in for a hug hoping it will calm him down.

Lucky goes "There are times I want to cry and I don't know why. My mind is not letting me think."

"I can't think and I forget who I am and where I am." says Lucky. "It's okay dear I'm here to help you, express how you feel." Goes his mom as she checks if he has a fever.

"Go lay down and see if you feel better." Lucky's mom is hoping he doesn't have a seizure. He walks away as she keeps her eyes on him.

Lucky is wondering where dad is so he goes looking for him. 'He is not in the living room so where might he be?' Lucky thinks to himself.

Lucky's dad comes into the living room and finds him on the couch. He can tell that something is wrong. "What's going on bud?"

"Dad I feel fuzzy and my arm is jumping a bit and I can't stop it." Says Lucky pointing to his arm.

"Dad it's falling asleep" continues Lucky as his dad now tries to calm him down by starting a breathing exercise.

"What should I do?" Says Lucky. His dad got up like superman. "I have an idea."

"Lucky try breathing in and out the way I taught you to." Says his father as they strike yoga poses.

"Okay let me breathe in and out." Says Lucky as he starts his breathing.

Thanks dad! I feel much better but still a little fuzzy. Should I go lay down?" "Yes, that should help you feel better Lucky"

Lucky went on to his room.

"I feel much better now. My mind is clear there is no doubt."

"Mommy and daddy always make me feel better." Says Lucky out loud.

'I am safe, secure and understood.' Thinks Lucky to himself as he is dozing off.

About the Author

Josie Martinez is an epilepsy warrior who's been dealing with her condition since she was 16. She has always had a passion for writing and wanting to help others. This book is only the beginning of what's to come on her journey.

Made in United States
North Haven, CT
26 June 2022

20654176R00022